Helping Dogs

by Linda Cernak

Harcourt

Orlando   Boston   Dallas   Chicago   San Diego

Visit *The Learning Site!*

www.harcourtschool.com

Many people have dogs as pets. Did you know that some people have dogs that are trained to help them?

Guide dogs lead people who are blind. A blind person is someone who cannot see. These dogs are trained to help blind people in their everyday lives.

Meet Pongo. She is getting an early checkup to see if she can train as a guide dog. Guide dogs must be strong and have good eyes. They will serve as the eyes of a person who is blind.

At two months old, Pongo goes to live with a family. She will stay for about a year to learn good manners.

Pongo's puppy raiser teaches her many things. She learns to walk on a leash. She gets used to going into shops and on buses. A guide dog must be able to lead a blind person anywhere.

Like all pups, Pongo seems to sprout quickly. When she is full grown, she goes back to the training school.

Pongo will be fitted with a harness that has a handle on it. The handle is a tool for the blind person. Holding it, he or she can feel which way the dog goes. Pongo learns to walk alongside her trainer.

Pongo learns to obey commands.
Trainers teach the dogs commands such as
"Right," "Left," and "Forward."

   Dogs learn to keep their minds on the job
while they are in harness. They must not stop
to go after a toy, food, or even a cat. They earn
praise for good work.

   Pongo learns these skills first in the
training school. Soon she will go out and train
in the real world.

Pongo learns how to cross a street. She listens and looks for cars. Pongo hears a car engine and knows it is not safe to cross. A guide dog must know when it is safe to lead a blind person off the curb.

Teaching a guide dog its important skills is not simple. Pongo must learn to handle busy traffic and wide street crossings. She will even learn how to lead a person around a mall!

Dogs learn how to lead safely up and down stairs. They will know how to lead their companion on and off buses and trains.

Unlike other dogs, these special dogs will go into stores and work places. They will need to know how to get around anywhere their companion wants to go.

After three months of training, it is time
for the dogs to pass the final test.

The test is hard, but Pongo and the others have learned well. They will be good guide dogs. Pongo's trainer is very pleased with her.

Now Pongo and the other dogs will train for one more month with their new owners. Trainers spend much time finding the right match of person and dog.

Today Pongo meets Ken for the first time. Ken spends time getting to know Pongo. He is so happy to have Pongo at his side. Ken knows that Pongo will help him do many things that he could not do alone. He also knows that Pongo will be his friend.

Pongo's day is not all about working. At night, Ken and Pongo have finished their day's chores. They can sit back and enjoy the friendship they share. They will be together for many years to come.